The Cheeky Pandas® Activity Book

Developed from an original idea by Pete James

Based on original designs and initial television artwork
by Noah Warnes and Missional Generation

Published by **Candle Books**
www.lionhudson.com
Part of the SPCK Group
SPCK, 36 Causton Street, London, SW1P 4ST

ISBN 978-1-78128-457-5

First edition 2023

Acknowledgments
Designed by aitch:creative ltd. www.aitchcreative.co.uk
Artwork from animations by Three Arrows Media

A catalogue record for this book is available
from The British Library

Produced on paper from sustainable sources
Printed and bound in China, November 2022, LH54

The Cheeky Pandas® Activity Book FOR KIDS!

Dot-to-dots, mazes,
spot the difference puzzles, and more!

by **Pete James**

CANDLE
BOOKS

The Cheeky Pandas live in a **treehouse music studio,**
can you find...

a slide

a chimney

a panda flag

a funnel

a swing

Answers on page 22

The Cheeky Pandas are playing hide and seek in the studio. Can you find them?

Benji

Lulu

Milo

CJ

Rory

Answers on page 22

The cheeky Pandas are rocking out!
Fill in the pictures to complete them.

LuLu sings the songs.

Milo plays the guitar.

Rory is DJ on the party mixer.

CJ plays the trombone.

Benji plays the drums.

What do the Cheeky Pandas use to order Packages from Pandaroo delivery?
Join the dots to find out.

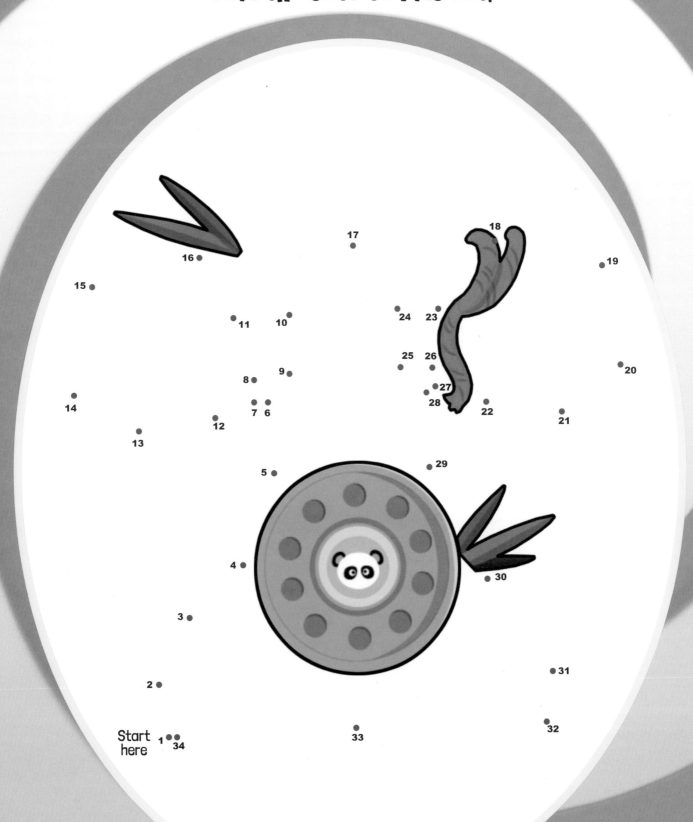

Start here

Find the way
for the Pandaroo
delivery van to reach
the cheeky Pandas'
treehouse.

Start here

PANDAROO

Answer on page 22

What have the cheeky pandas ordered from Pandaroo delivery?
Match the packages to the objects inside.

Answers on page 22

The Cheeky Pandas **love bouncing** on the **bouncy castle.**

Use the code to complete the picture.

1	2	3
red	yellow	blue

Start here

Oh no! The robot lawnmower is **chasing Rory** on his skateboard.

Follow the robot lawnmower through the maze.

Answer on page 23

Can you spot the five differences
between the two pictures
of the Cheeky Pandas in the garden?

Answer on page 23

What instrument does Milo LOVE to play?

Join the dots to find out.

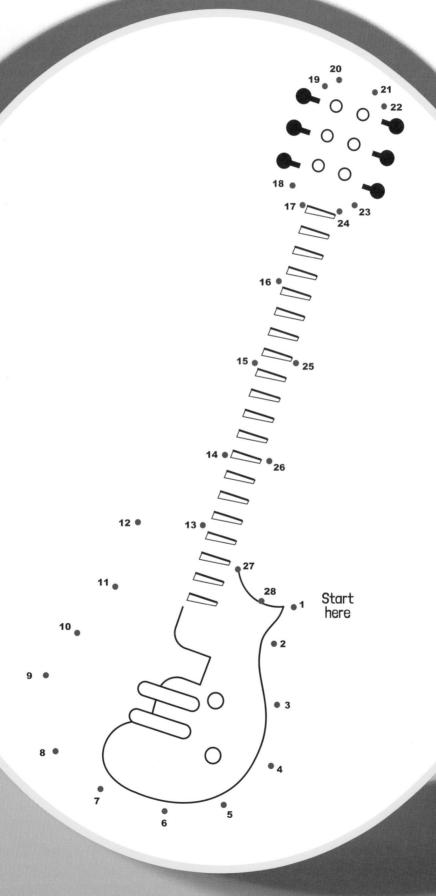

There are **five pairs** of matching Milos – Draw a line to match up the pairs.

The first one has been done for you.

Answers on page 23

The Cheeky Pandas have been given some disco lights from their record label.

Can you find...

paint brushes

a cymbal

a yellow guitar

a Pandamonia book

a small plant

Answers on page 23

With God's help, the cheeky Pandas try to be
loving joyful patient kind faithful
can you find these words?

d	r	x	j	q	a	g	q	u	c
g	k	z	j	y	k	a	p	k	v
q	e	g	t	v	i	h	a	r	v
j	d	z	k	k	n	y	t	l	o
o	a	e	s	n	d	i	i	o	q
y	j	x	a	s	l	h	e	v	s
f	l	n	f	b	x	d	n	i	m
u	o	q	g	i	u	k	t	n	u
l	k	n	f	x	r	p	h	g	a
j	n	f	a	i	t	h	f	u	l

Answers on page 23

To the song machine!

Fill in the picture to complete it.

SONG MACHINE 400   0

Answers

Page 4

Page 5

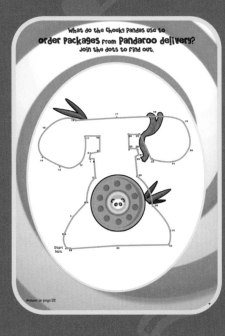

Page 11

Page 12

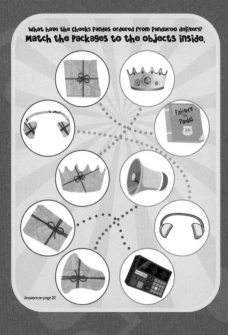

Page 13

Page 14

Oh no! The robot lawnmower is chasing Rory on his skateboard.

Start here

Follow the robot lawnmower through the maze.

Answer on page 23

Page 15

Can you spot the five differences between the two pictures of the Cheeky Pandas in the garden?

Answer on page 23

Page 16

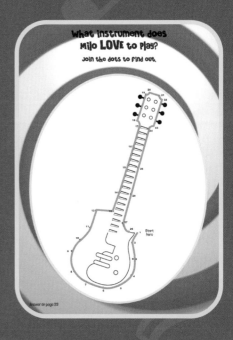

What instrument does Milo LOVE to play?

Join the dots to find out.

Start here

Answer on page 23

Page 17

There are 5 pairs of matching Milos – draw a line to match up the pairs.

The first one has been done for you.

Answers on page 23

Page 18

The cheeky pandas have been given some disco lights from their record label.

Can you find...

Paint brushes

a cymbal

a yellow guitar

a Pandamonia book

a small plant

Answers on page 23

Page 19

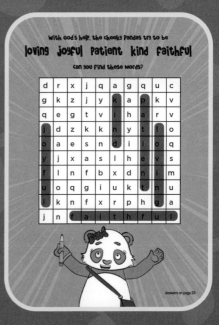

With God's help, the cheeky pandas try to be

loving joyful patient kind faithful

Can you find these words?

d	r	x	j	q	a	g	q	u	c
g	k	z	j	y	k	a	p	k	v
q	e	g	t	v	i	h	a	r	v
j	d	z	k	k	n	y	t	l	o
o	a	e	s	n	d	i	i	o	q
y	j	x	a	s	l	h	e	v	s
f	l	n	f	b	x	d	n	i	m
u	o	q	g	i	u	k	t	n	u
i	k	n	f	x	r	p	h	g	a
j	n	f	a	i	t	h	f	u	l

Answers on page 23

Page 20

23

About the Cheeky Pandas®

Cheeky Pandas® provide free online resources to help children and families grow in their faith.
The songs, music videos, episodes, and devotionals are fun, bright, professionally written and produced.
Families, churches, and ministries around the world can access and directly watch these resources.

To hear the songs from the song machine and to
watch the full animated episodes go to:

www.cheekypandas.com

Why not Pick uP a Cheeky Pandas® storybook?

The Bouncy Castle
ISBN 978 1 78128 455 1

The Best Present Ever
ISBN 978 1 78128 452 0

The Day Off
ISBN 978 1 78128 453 7

The Drum Machine
ISBN 978-1-78128-456-8

The Lost Voice
ISBN 978-1-78128-459-9

Goodbye Pandas!

Until your next adventure.